AS HOGAN SAID...

The 389 Best Things Anyone Said About How to Play Golf

Compiled and Edited by
Randy Voorhees

A MOUNTAIN LION BOOK
Published by Simon & Schuster
New York · London · Toronto · Sydney · Singapore

SIMON & SCHUSTER
Rockefeller Center
1230 Avenue of the Americas
New York, NY 10020

Manufactured in the United States of America

10   9   8   7   6

Library of Congress Cataloging-in-Publication Data
As Hogan said— : the 389 best things anyone said about
how to play golf / compiled and edited by Randy Voorhees.
p. cm.
"A Mountain Lion book."
1. Golfers—Quotations. 2. Golf—Quotations, maxims, etc.
3. Golf—Humor. I. Title: 389 best things anyone said about
how to play golf. II. Voorhees, Randy.
GV967 .A82 2000
796.352—dc21   00-061235
ISBN 0-7432-0376-3

Acknowledgments

If what we know now of golf and of golfers has always been true, then the very first golf quotation was most likely unprintable. I feel safe in saying this, because it was undoubtedly uttered well before the development of printing itself. The first written reference to golf dates back to 1457—just two years after Johannes Gutenberg put out his own version of the Rules—when the Parliament of King James II ordered that "Fute-ball and Golfe be utterly cryed down." We can be sure that much time had been spent crying over the game by then.

In seeking to pull together the thoughts and wisdom contained in these pages, I drew inspiration from Robert Byrnes's classic compilation of quotations, *The 637 Best Things Anybody Ever Said.* Everyone who plays golf can quote a hundred useless things they've heard about the game: "Keep your left arm straight." "Never up, never in." "All putts break toward the ocean." "A tree is 90 percent air." So why not offer the long-suffering golfer some intelligent, useful, accurate advice instead?

In the beginning I thought compiling the quotations for this book would be a simple task. Golf is mysterious, frustrating, challenging, addictive—all characteristics that make for profound and timeless utterances, right? Well, yes and no.

Yes, if you're willing to spend hours and days digging through the writings of the great players and writers of the late nineteenth and early twentieth centuries. Men such as Harry Vardon, Horace Hutchinson, Sir Walter Simpson, James Braid, and Jerome Travers, to name just a few, had many interesting things to say about the best way to play golf. Best of all, they did their own writing, so their distinctive personalities and beliefs shone through. You won't find words such as "supination" or "pronation" in their manuscripts.

On the other hand, it was difficult—hell, nearly impossible—to find quotations from contemporary players that could survive the final cut. I don't think this means that golfers such as Tiger Woods and David Duval don't have anything important or insightful to say; I think it means that writers don't often get an opportunity to sit around while Tiger and David wax philosophic or expound upon the virtues of a flat wrist at impact. If you're looking for a pearl from one of the young guns, you will probably have to look elsewhere. But if you believe that the value of gems owes little to their youth, and cherish wisdom that has stood the test of time, then this is the book for you.

My sincere hope is that you will find this collection

Acknowledgments

entertaining and informative. Your game may well improve because of it. If so, before you report the details to me or to the publisher, please review the words of Horace Hutchinson as contained in Section Two.

I would like to offer my thanks to my colleagues, Mark Gola and John Monteleone, for contributing several gems, and for their support. Thanks, too, to Jeff Neuman at Simon & Schuster for allowing me to compile this book, and to his associate, Andrew Cohen, for sending me plenty of resource material. Last, though certainly not least, my sincere appreciation to Rand Jerris, the head librarian and historian for the United States Golf Association, for being a gracious host during the research phase of this project.

To be sure, there are many wonderful quotations that I didn't include in this volume, and that's either because they didn't survive the winnowing process or I didn't find them. If it's the latter, then I welcome your help. If you have a favorite or six that I've overlooked, please drop me a line or a postcard c/o Mountain Lion, Inc., 197 Wall Street, Princeton, NJ 08540 and I'll try and find a good home for them. Thanks.

Randy Voorhees
Princeton, New Jersey

For my girls,
Sarah and Carol.

Contents

Contents

AS HOGAN SAID...

SECTION 1

It's Only a Game

THE GAME

It's not your life, it's not your wife, it's only a game.

—*Lloyd Mangrum*

It takes longer to kill the golf in a man than it does to breed it.

—*Harry Vardon*

Golf is very healthy; it is better to swat pills than to swallow them.

—*Ted Osborne*

Tennis players don't sleep in parking lots on Saturday night.

—*David Owen*

Confidence, of course, is an admirable asset to a golfer, but it should be an unspoken confidence. It is perilous to put it into speech. The gods of golf lie in wait to chasten the presumptuous.

—*P. G. Wodehouse*

The Game

People often ask me, "Why can't I play golf the same every day?" Well, what can you do the same every day? I don't even get out of bed the same way.

—*Jackie Burke, Jr.*

Few things draw two men together more surely than a mutual inability to master golf, coupled with an intense and ever-increasing love for the game.

—*P. G. Wodehouse*

Most of us have a real warped idea of the amount of control we have over anything. It's not that we can't control certain aspects of this game, it's that we think we can control everything. That's where our error is. Then God says, "Wait a minute, just so you don't forget." A fleck of grass throws a putt off-line, the ball is stuck in a tree or shoots this way or that. The elements, variables, the unexpected. That's golf.

—*Annette Thompson*

Golf teaches success and failure. Neither lasts long.

—*Glenn Kummer*

Three things are as unfathomable as they are fascinating: metaphysics, golf, and the feminine heart. The Germans, I believe, pretend to have solved some of the riddles of the first, and the French to have unravelled some of the intricacies of the last; will someone tell us wherein lies the extraordinary fascination of golf?

—Arnold Haultain

There is no type of miracle that can't happen at least once in golf.

—Grantland Rice

On the golf course, a man may be the dogged victim of inexorable fate, be struck down by an appalling stroke of tragedy, become the hero of unbelievable melodrama, or the clown in a side-splitting comedy.

—Bobby Jones

In golf you've got two continuously merciless competitors: yourself and the course.

—Tommy Armour

The trouble with all of us, who grumble over the game and thus spoil an otherwise pleasant afternoon with congenial

The Game

friends, is that we do not understand the game, nor ourselves. In this, we could take a number of lessons from the [hacker]. For no matter how good we may be, if we should fancy that we have mastered golf to the extent that we can go out day after day and play as we please, then we are greater fools than ought to be left at large.

—Bobby Jones

> A good round of golf is if you can hit
> about three shots that turn out exactly as
> you planned them.
>
> *—Ben Hogan*

The score is important, of course. And the discovery that you are superior to another golfer is satisfying. But when your score is bad and the other fellow beats you, golf still has been a blessing to you. The score isn't the "be all and end all."

—Tommy Armour

There is no shape nor size of body, no awkwardness nor ungainliness, which puts good golf beyond reach. There are good golfers with spectacles, with one eye, with one leg, even with one arm. In golf, while there is life there is hope.

—Sir Walter Simpson

The mere test of strength or of skill is one of the most subordinate of the elements of golf; much more important is the test of what goes by the name of "nerve," that quiet self-confidence which no ghastly phantasms can shake. . . . So many golfers forget this. "If I had not done this, that, or the other stupid thing," they say, "my score would have been so-and-so." My dear sir, it is just those stupid things that make the game.

—Arnold Haultain

SECTION 2

There Are No Born Golfers

STARTING OUT

Rest assured, there are no "born golfers." Those who have made headway went through the process of seeking and finding and forged ahead after deep diggings on many fairways.

—*Glenna Collett Vare*

A golfer who learns to swing hard initially can usually acquire accuracy later, whereas a golfer who gets too accuracy-conscious at the outset will rarely be able to make himself hit the ball hard later on.

—*Jack Nicklaus*

Seve Ballesteros was immensely lucky when he started playing golf. There wasn't a golf instruction book within miles of his home in northern Spain. True, he was in some jeopardy from his elder brother, Manuel, who was a tournament pro, but some native instinct saved Seve from seeking advice or listening to any hints which were volunteered in his direction. The youngster learned how to hit the ball by subconsciously absorbing the example of good players and translating these images into violent action on a trial-and-error basis.

—*Golf Digest*

Starting Out

The wise man who has respect for the game before he plays it will take as much advice and coaching as he can get, and he will be content to begin in the most elementary way, and will not mind any amount of practice before he tries to make a complete round of the links.

—James Braid

The only club in the bag specifically designed to get the ball in the cup is the putter. Why not learn it first?

—Jackie Burke, Jr.

I believe the natural, logical, and easiest way to teach golf is to start with the shortest swing and then increase it to a full swing. I strongly believe it's much easier to learn golf's basic elements—aiming the clubface and hitting the ball consistently in the middle of the clubface—by using a short rather than a long swing.

—Tom Watson

The younger you are, the more you should focus on your short game. It is hard to have a perfect golf swing when you are fourteen or fifteen years old because you are not done growing yet. But that touch you develop by working on your short game will stick with you your entire life.

—Bob Estes

Golf should be learned starting at the cup and progressing back toward the tee. . . . If a beginner tries to learn the game at the tee and move on toward the green, postponing the short game until last, this is one beginner who will be lucky to ever beat anybody.

—Harvey Penick

Every beginner ought to play with golfers better than himself. He will unconsciously by that means aim higher. It should be his ambition to beat somebody, and, having done so, to attack a still stronger adversary.

—Sir Walter Simpson

The friend who introduced you to the Royal and Ancient Game may indeed evince some interest in your progress, as is but proper as he is your father in golf, but you really must not expect every golfer of your acquaintance to listen very attentively to your detailed account of all incidents of your round. If you are too prolix, you must not be surprised if

some of your friends are almost tempted to hope that your
first round may also be your last.

—Horace Hutchinson

Golf, like the measles, should be caught young, for, if
postponed to riper years, the results may be serious.

—P. G. Wodehouse

If you really want to get better at golf, go
back and take it up at a much earlier age.

—Henry Beard

In golf, as in other sports, youth is a great helper, but if you
cannot start at three, or twelve, or even thirty-five, start at
forty-five or fifty. Remember that it's better to have golfed
and foozled than never golfed at all.

—Jerome Travers

When you play golf, just play golf. Here's you, here's the
ball, there's the target. Go to it. Hit the ball to the target as
best you can. Find the ball and do it again. Experience, adjust, experience, adjust. . . . The golf course is made for playing a game! So go there and *play* golf.

—Chuck Hogan

EQUIPMENT

The trouble that most of us find with the modern matched sets of clubs is that they don't really seem to know any more about the game than the old ones did.

—Robert Browning

Let us consider the equipment we have to use. A more ill-designed set of implements could hardly have been created. Yet we descend upon each new model with cries of glee, drooling over the gleaming heads.

—Chris Plumbridge

You can't go into a shop and buy a good
game of golf.

—Sam Snead

One may well begin with the positive assurance that no first-class ball is as much as twenty yards, or even fifteen yards, longer than any other first-class ball. This difference, on the driving machine, is rarely more than two or three yards on the carry.

—Bobby Jones

Equipment

Armed with ignorance, golfers shell out hundreds, sometimes thousands of dollars on new clubs, believing that their investment is going to help them play better. You can spend a million dollars; if your clubs don't fit, you're not going to play good golf.

—Jonathan Abrahams

Properly fitted clubs are the only part of improved golf that anyone can buy.

—Tommy Armour

The modern player has grown so accustomed to having a special club for every conceivable stroke that he fails to realize how much his vaunted skill is due to the science of the clubmakers, who have introduced limber shafts to give him greater strength, lofted clubs to put stop on his approach shots, and sand wedges of amazing design to dig him out of bunkers that a better man would never have got into.

—Robert Browning

Golfers who carry ball retrievers are gatherers, not hunters. . . . Their dreams are no longer of conquest, but only of salvage.

—David Owen

I suppose the great value of a bag of odd clubs is that there will always be two or three which feel right on any particular day. With a perfectly matched set they are either all in or all out.

—Henry Cotton

The best way to tell whether any golf gadget will help your game is to try to picture Fred Couples using it.

—Henry Beard

If I catch one of my amateur friends playing with a one-iron, he had better be putting with it.

—Tommy Bolt

Surprising how few golfers ever carry two putters, yet it seems logical, for one has more strokes with a putter than any other club in every round, or in fact, any two clubs together and a switch during a round might do wonders.

—Henry Cotton

Some players are never satisfied unless they are buying new clubs. . . . This is not good for the player, but it is quite good for the clubmaker.

—James Braid

Equipment

Maybe the number of clubs we carry is less important than the selection. Five clubs may truly be all I need—as long as none of the five is a driver, a long iron, or the elusive Unhittable Club of the Day, which moves unpredictably around my golf bag.

—David Owen

In playing golf for more than 50 years, I don't believe there ever was a round in which I used more than six clubs. . . . Today there's a stick in the sack for every shot. . . . Golfers used to be made on the golf courses. Now they are made in the machine shops.

—Donald Ross

The pet club is a necessary institution. But it must not be catered to out of reason. It must be kept, at least partially, in its place. There are certain large moments when it must be rushed to the rescue of fluttering nerves and fading hopes. But don't let these moments occur too often. Being slave to a game is one thing. Being a cringing captive to one warped club is something else.

—Grantland Rice

BREAKING THROUGH

Well, if you want to see a radical improvement in your game and cut off five strokes in a week or two, you must make a radical change in the way you practice. For two weeks devote 90 percent of your practice time to chipping and putting, and only 10 percent to the full swing. If you do this, your 95 will turn into 90. I guarantee it.

—Harvey Penick

To break 90, mentally remove every pin and instead concentrate on hitting greens. Take dead aim at the center of each green. Do this from every distance outside 50 yards.

—Jim McLean

What separates the great players from the good players or the 15-handicap player from the 20-handicap player is not so much ability as brainpower and emotional equilibrium.

—Arnold Palmer

Consider, if you will, that on a par-72 course you can bogey 17 of the 18 holes and still break 90.

—Cliff McAdams

Breaking Through

> There is no other sphere in which a belief
> in oneself has such immediate effects as
> it has in golf.
>
> —*P. G. Wodehouse*

To break 100, you must focus on the short game. Rule number one of your short game goes something like this: *minimum air time, maximum ground time.* Rule number two: putt whenever you can, even if you're not on the green. When you can't putt, chip. When you can't chip, pitch.

> —*Mike Adams and
> T. J. Tomasi*

If everybody could learn to hold his head still there wouldn't be any golfers around still trying to break 100.

> —*Arnold Palmer*

LESSONS

I never quite understood the idea of those seeking to standardize golf instruction throughout the world. It was perhaps in theory a worthwhile idea, but one destined to fail. While I am prepared to concede there are certain fundamentals in the golf swing, I believe the whole art of teaching golf lies in helping the pupil to translate the fundamental principles via his own physique.

—Henry Cotton

I always tell my students that if there is a road to good golf, nowhere on that road is there a slice. You can go from hooking to good golf. You can go from slicing to hooking to good golf. But you can't go from slicing to good golf.

—Hank Haney

It amazes me how many people resist taking golf lessons. They feel they don't need instruction, like they're some kind of lesser athlete if they can't figure out this game by themselves. If you're one of these people, remember that Michael Jordan and John Elway were coached every day of their careers. Don't be so darned stubborn.

—Dr. Richard Coop

A lesson is of very short duration, but will, if properly understood, provide you with tasks for a week or more.

—Henry Cotton

Lessons

You learn golf all the time, but you don't
learn it all at once

—Davis Love, Jr.

The player who is anxious to improve must be prepared
to exchange unsound methods for sound ones, and in the
period of transition to bear the annoyance and humil-
iation of being unable to produce his previous best for
the sake of producing afterwards a best which is very
much better.

—Henry Cotton

Innumerable times I've had golfers come to me complaining about some fault that is ruining their swings. . . . A
goodly number of these victims will begin telling me
what's wrong with their swings. They don't seem to realize
that if they knew what was wrong, they wouldn't be com-
ing to me and paying me for an expert diagnosis and cure.

—Tommy Armour

The player who expects a lesson to "take" without subse-
quent practice just isn't being honest with himself or fair
to his professional.

—Gary Player

There are three ways of learning golf: by study, which is the most wearisome; by imitation, which is the most fallacious; and by experience, which is the most bitter.

—Robert Browning

The first really practical method of teaching is of course personal instruction, where both the teacher and the pupil have a club in hand, and one can illustrate and correct, the other repeat and swear.

—Bobby Jones

The good players are almost always the ones who ask me to watch them on the putting green. The high-handicappers, who need it the most, would rather do anything than have a putting lesson.

—Harvey Penick

"Never had a lesson in my life" is a phrase uttered with smug satisfaction by a good many people. The correct reply is, of course, "That's why you are no better than you are."

—Henry Longhurst

PRACTICE

Every day you don't hit balls is one day
longer it takes you to get better.

> —*Ben Hogan*

Practice is the only golf advice that is
good for everybody.

> —*Arnold Palmer*

The average golfer would rather play
above 100 than face what he thinks is the
drudgery of practice.

> —*Grantland Rice*

The harder I practice the luckier I get.

> —*Gary Player*

All my life I've tried to hit practice shots with great care.
I try to have a clear-cut purpose in mind on every swing. I
always practice as I intend to play. And I learned long ago
that there is a limit to the number of shots you can hit ef-

fectively before losing your concentration on your basic objectives.

—*Jack Nicklaus*

Never practice your full swing when the wind is blowing at your back. If you're right-handed, this means the wind is left to right. The more you practice with the wind blowing left to right, the more you will be inclined to swing across the ball and hit from the top.

—*Harvey Penick*

Always practice to a target, keeping the pile of balls some distance away so you take your time between swings. Play the course on the range.

—*Gary Player*

It isn't the *hours* you put in at practice that count. It's the way you spend those *minutes.*

—*Tony Lema*

I figure practice puts brains in your muscles.

—*Sam Snead*

Practice

If you can only sneak a little time each week to practice, work on your alignment. Lay some clubs on the ground to use as a guide; that way your swing can develop around a solid setup position.

—*Billy Ray Brown*

No one should know your swing better than you do. That's why I've been working with a camera on my swing since 1960. When people ask me who my teacher is I say, "Sony," because the camera does not lie. I check for little things starting to creep into my swing so I can catch them before they become big problems.

—*Jimmy Powell*

The secret's in the dirt. Dig it out like I did.

—*Ben Hogan*

The practice tee is the place to try things out and to work hard; the golf course is the place to let things go, free yourself up. Don't try harder on the golf course. Try *less* hard.

—*Davis Love, Jr.*

The most valuable time to practice is right after your round, when your mistakes are fresh in your mind.

—Tom Watson

Go find some stimulating, fulfilling, challenging human endeavor that, unlike golf, does not require a commitment of time and effort to realize maximum enjoyment. And call me when you find it.

—Jim Flick

No golfer can ever become too good to practice.

—May Hezlet

SECTION 3

*Learn the Game
from the Green to the Tee*

PUTTING

The man who can putt is a match for anyone.

—*Willie Park, Jr.*

If there's one thing certain about putting, it is that it's an individual business. The great putters have used every conceivable type of grip, stance and stroke.

—*Ben Crenshaw*

The overwhelming majority of unsuccessful putts are missed not because they were misjudged but because they were mis-hit.

—*Jackie Burke, Jr.*

The stroke must be made with rhythm. The change of direction should be smooth and unforced, just as it is with the pendulum of a grandfather clock.

—*Tom Watson*

Putting

It is not necessary to go back and through
the same length. That's hogwash, unless
it happens to work for you.

—*Jim McLean*

When a putter is waiting his turn to hole out a putt of one
or two feet in length, on which the match hangs at the
last hole, it is of vital importance that he think of
nothing. At this supreme moment he ought to fill his
mind with vacancy. He must not even allow himself the
consolations of religion.

—*Sir Walter Simpson*

The chief reaction among amateurs to poor putting, it
seems to me, is exasperation, combined with a sort of
vague hope that, by some kind of mini-miracle, it will all
have gotten better by the next time they play.

—*Jack Nicklaus*

The proper putting stroke cannot be contrived or manipulated with the hands—it
must be natural.

—*Ben Crenshaw*

There is no tragedy in missing a putt, no matter how short. We have all erred in this respect. Short putts are missed because it is not physically possible to make the little ball travel over uncertain ground for three or four feet with any degree of regularity.

—Walter Hagen

Many amateurs hit a putt too hard and turn away in disgust as the ball passes the hole. I watch closely as a putt goes by the hole to see how the comeback putt will break.

—Tom Watson

If a putt looks straight, don't stare at the line for a long period of time trying to see if there's something you overlooked. Sooner or later, you'll invent a break that isn't there.

—Corey Pavin

The majority treat the hole as a place more difficult to get into than it really is. . . . The hole is pretty big, and from all distances is capable of catching a ball going at a fair pace. Many more putts would go in if players credited holes with a little of that catching power which they really possess.

—Sir Walter Simpson

Putting

The golfer who makes the best score has *always* done some very good putting.

—George Low

The devoted golfer is an anguished soul who has learned a lot about putting just as an avalanche victim has learned a lot about snow.

—Dan Jenkins

To the beginner putting seems the least interesting part of the game. Like other things, essentially foolish in themselves, such as preaching, putting becomes attractive in proportion to the skill acquired in it.

—Sir Walter Simpson

I have never seen a pocket billiards player lose his stroke. He's not thinking about his stroke. He's thinking about what's in front of him, as athletes in other sports do. His concern is moving the cue ball to a certain point with a certain amount of speed, not how he's holding the darn cue stick.

—Roger Maltbie

Forget the silly notion, preached by some, that there is any virtue in half-topping, or up-hitting, or in any other device designed to impart overspin.

—*Bobby Jones*

All things being equal, greens break to the west.

—*Harvey Penick*

I work to the rule that if the green appears to be fast, I will aim my putt at an imaginary hole six to twelve inches short of the hole. If the green appears to be slow, and particularly if during the last two or three feet to the hole the ground is uphill, I hit it firmly for the back of the hole.

—*Bobby Locke*

Golfers who don't care never get the yips.

—*Dave Pelz*

Every now and then I run into a putting slump. I experiment with different clubs and different styles. The one thing I don't change is my belief that I am going to regain my touch.

—*Arnold Palmer*

Putting

After you stroke a putt, the only thing you can do is listen for it to fall in. You're not going to gain anything by peeking.

—*Dr. Cary Middlecoff*

Accurate putting is impossible when the body is swayed. And keep your eye on the ball, not looking forward anxiously to the hole just as the club hits the ball. This is a very human but very fatal fault, and it costs many holes to those who make it.

—*James Braid*

If there is one constant I've found for being successful on the greens, it's that good putters believe they are good putters.

—*Raymond Floyd*

All those who drive thirty yards suppose themselves to be great putters.

—*Sir Walter Simpson*

When the ball dies at the hole there are four doors; the ball can go in the front, or the back, or at either side. But a ball that comes up to the hole with speed on it must hit the front door in the middle; there are no side doors, and no Sunday entrance.

—*Stewart Maiden*

The thing that hurt my putting most was thinking too much about how I was making the stroke, and not enough about getting the ball into the hole.

—*Bobby Jones*

Taking the high road—playing more break rather than less—makes sense for many reasons: A ball is more likely to fall down into the hole from the high side than fall up from the low side; it also encourages rolling the ball at a slower speed, meaning it is less likely to run too far past the hole should it miss.

—*Dave Pelz*

The average golfer needs to realize that rolling a ten-footer up to the front edge of the cup is to be applauded, not sneered at. The only time I can imagine when it would be dreadfully wrong to leave a putt short is if you must sink it to win the match or the tournament or the skin.

—*Harvey Penick*

Putting

Far more putts are missed because of incorrect distance than incorrect direction.

—John Jacobs

Bad putting stems from thinking *how* instead of *where.*

—Jackie Burke, Jr.

The most important shot in golf is the 6-foot putt. If you're sound from 6 feet, you've widened your target for chips, pitches and lag-putts to a 12-foot circle, a nice, comfortable target. You can't spend too much time practicing 6-footers.

—Raymond Floyd

I'll do *anything* to make a putt.

—Jack Nicklaus

Putting is still a black art. There is no right way to putt. Good putters have feel or touch, and do not ask me what that means, or why it happens, because nobody knows. One day you've got it and the next time out the putter hefts like a sledgehammer in your hands and you can't even threaten the hole.

—Peter Dobereiner

Because the green has so many variables—fast, slow, up-hill, downhill, sidehill, against the grain, with the grain, cross-grained—when you work on putting, you're working on the sensitivity, feel, and creativity that is needed all over the course.

—Jim Flick

CHIPPING AND PITCHING

Around the green, play the club that keeps the ball nearest to the ground. It's easier to roll the ball up to the hole than fly the ball up and stop it by the hole. Putt rather than chip, and chip rather than pitch.

—Billy Casper

The shorter the shot the more deliberate and carefully thought out your efforts must be.

—Henry Longhurst

Poor chipping is the primary reason the handicap of the average golfer has remained frozen.

—Corey Pavin

Chipping and Pitching

To have a good chipping game you must aim to hit a spot. This is a necessary addition to your regular preshot checklist. You check all the variables and decide what type of chip to hit. Then you must pick the spot for the ball to land, and visualize the ball landing there and running to the hole.

—*Johnny Miller*

The great anxiety of the moderate player when making his stroke is to get the ball properly lofted, and in some obstinate cases it seems to take several seasons of experience to convince him completely that the club has been specially made for the purpose, and, if fairly used, is quite adequate.

—*Harry Vardon*

The common error is taking the club back too far and decelerating through impact, which is like a boxer pulling his punches. It causes all sorts of mishit and misdirected pitch shots.

—*Tom Watson*

It is demonstrably more difficult to control a shot with a club of extreme loft than with one of moderate pitch. Therefore, the clubs of extreme loft should be left in the bag until the need for them becomes well defined.

—*Bobby Jones*

Distance control is critical in pitching. One of the benefits of *light grip pressure* is increased sensitivity in your hands, which in turn provides the intuitive sense for how far the ball will fly on a given pitch.

—Corey Pavin

If the average guy hits five or six greens that means he must miss at least twelve. Of those, maybe four times he can chip his ball onto the putting surface. Which leaves eight pitch shots. Other than driving or putting, that makes pitching the most important shot in your bag.

—Hank Haney

Distance, distance, distance. I cannot stress it enough. Know what a 40-yard shot is. Know a 20-yard shot. A 60-yard shot. Get that down. Not every golfer can hit the ball as far as Tiger Woods or as relentlessly straight as Ben Hogan did. But any golfer can hit the ball 40 yards. Learn how to use that wedge.

—Roger Maltbie

Here's another way to look at the importance of the short game to your overall handicap. You can't do much to recover after hitting a bad pitch or chip shot, while you often can recover from poor longer shots. Just like a poor putt, a poor pitch or chip shot is usually another shot lost to par.

—*Dave Pelz*

It is my opinion that all chip shots and pitch shots should be played to carry on to the putting surface *in the air,* thereby eliminating any chance of the ball hitting some bump or depression in the turf and taking a bad kick.

—*Dr. Cary Middlecoff*

There should be no excessive wrist action for this [chipping] stroke. The simplest, most straightforward way to play these shots is without spin. With shorter chip shots, you do this by taking your wrists out of the shot. Try not cocking your wrists.

—*Ben Crenshaw*

Roll is easier to judge than flight.

—*Jack Nicklaus*

The Texas Wedge is strictly a percentage shot. Perhaps it's not so beautiful to behold as the delicate chip. But if you'd rather *be* a golfer than merely look like one, the

Texas Wedge will save you a stroke in seven or eight out of every ten chip shots.

—*Jackie Burke, Jr.*

Since it is beyond all reasonable expectations that a person may hole a chip shot, little will be gained by playing always for the hole. . . . There are times when a four-foot uphill putt is a far less annoying proposition than one of half that length across a keen slope.

—*Bobby Jones*

When I was a youngster, I played a wedge most of the time around the green. I'd try to hit a high, lofted shot up to the hole no matter where I was. I got away with it much of the time because I was young and had the nerves of a neurosurgeon. But I finally learned after too many "three to get down" holes to use different clubs to fit different shots.

—*Tom Watson*

If you think you can hole a chip shot, take out the flagstick, because the flagstick never helped a perfect shot.

—*Davis Love, Jr.*

SAND PLAY

No bunker shot has ever scared me, and none ever will. The key to this bravado is practice. I've practiced and experimented from hundreds of lies with various swings, in effect creating a data bank in my memory that I can call on no matter what kind of sand shot I'm facing. Just as important, I've developed my imagination to the point that I'm confident I can think my way out of any bunker, no matter how tough the lie.

—*Gary Player*

It is hard to judge the strength or thickness of the sand— a very important matter—because you are not allowed to touch the sand with your club. However, you can plant your feet firmly in the sand when addressing the ball, and after a little experience you will be able to estimate the strength of the sand by means of a pair of well-trained feet.

—*Jerome Travers*

I admit that it does appear unworkmanlike and amateurish to run a shot through sand and out of a bunker, but it sometimes becomes necessary to disregard appearances.

A few disasters resulting from a desire to display brilliant technique are enough to harden even the most sensitive nature. . . . Once the round is under way, the business at hand becomes that of getting results. Nothing else matters.

—Bobby Jones

One of the easiest ways to add height to the [sand] shot is to feel like you're sitting down on your right knee at address. You should widen your stance and choke up a little. You should feel as if you're "under" the ball more and have a wider base.

—Ben Crenshaw

Bunkers are not placed on a course haphazard, but they are made at particular places to catch particular kinds of defective shots.

—James Braid

Harvey Penick always wanted us to be good bunker players so we wouldn't be afraid to fire at a flag tucked next to one.

—Tom Kite

Sand Play

You must keep the clubface open in soft sand. I simply cannot stress enough the importance of this. My father used to make me imagine that I had a glass balanced on the clubface. The only way it could stay there was if the clubface remained open through the hitting area.

—Johnny Miller

One of the best practice drills from sand is to tee the ball low and then play the shot. Your goal is to try to break the tee in half.

—Corey Pavin

Remember that the object of most greenside bunker shots is not to "blast" the ball out, but to float it fairly gently from the trap on a cushion of sand, by skimming the club easily just beneath the ball.

—John Jacobs

Would you like to know the fastest way to take several strokes off your game? Spend two hours in a bunker.

—Greg Norman

I think the golfer who fails to clean up his mess in a sand trap should be banned from the game. . . . The absence of a rake is no excuse for not smoothing the sand. You can take care of the marks easily with the back of a club.

—*Jack Nicklaus*

The two mistakes I see most often from amateurs are lifting up and hitting the equator of the ball, sending it into the next county, or taking a divot of sand large enough to bury a cat.

—*Sam Snead*

FAIRWAY WOODS

Don't be too steep with your swing. You want to brush the grass, not take a divot. Swing the clubhead back on a wide arc and swing it through on a wide arc. Extend your left arm on the backswing and then extend your right arm on the through-swing. Think of swinging the clubhead wide to wide.

—*Tom Watson*

Fairway Woods

The real value of fairway woods is their
effectiveness from rough.

—Corey Pavin

Follow the lead of the Senior Tour and LPGA pros. They
use more fairway woods. Annika Sorenstam, one of the
best players in the world, has nothing longer than a
5-iron in her bag. She uses five fairway woods. Most
golfers should carry five woods; long irons are just too
hard to hit.

—Hank Haney

The size and the looks of the woods
alone are psychological aids and make
these clubs easier to use, by the average
player, than the long irons.

—Tommy Armour

A good 7-wood is not only easier to hit than a 3-iron, but
it's also a lot more versatile. You can play it from
medium-height rough or from an iffy lie in the fairway.
It's also easier to get a 7-wood airborne.

—Johnny Miller

To prevent slices and to give more distance, I teach pupils to hit the woods from a closed stance, with the right foot two or three inches farther back than the left. The good golfers hit their woods from slightly closed stances. The closed stance permits the hips and body to turn easily, and as much as is needed.

—*Tommy Armour*

As for the No. 3 wood, my experience is that too many players are not careful enough about examining the lie on the fairway before they use it. Somehow it has become the recognized thing to take [the] wood no matter how bad the lie. Only use [a] wood on the fairway if you have a really good lie.

—*Bobby Locke*

DRIVING

I'd say reasonably that 50 percent of the time the average player would do better to leave the driver in the bag and hit the 3-wood. The shorter club with more loft allows them to do two things: (1) not slice the ball as much and, (2) hit the center of the clubface more often. If you took the average distance of ten shots played with a driver and ten shots played with a 3-wood, you would probably find the 3-woods go as far or farther and definitely hit the fairway more often.

—Jim McLean

The higher the ball sits [on the tee], the more we tend to sweep it away with a somewhat flatter swing. This, in itself, generally squares the clubface a bit sooner in the hitting area.

—John Jacobs

The biggest challenge you face on the tee—even before you decide what kind of shot you want to hit—is changing your mind-set from "driving range" to "on the course."

—Johnny Miller

Whatever your natural ball flight, you can use it to your advantage, because *you can always eliminate one side of the golf course.* You can always start a reliable fade down the left side of the fairway, for example; whether it goes straight, fades slightly or fades a lot, *you're still in the fairway.* A draw works similarly from the right side.

—Jim McLean

The tee is the only place where you have the ball in hand and can decide for yourself where you want to play the shot from. By teeing the ball on the side of the teeing ground that best suits the shot you're playing, you widen the fairway.

—Corey Pavin

In the golf education of every man there is a definite point at which he may be said to have crossed the dividing line—the Rubicon, as it were—that separates the golfer from the non-golfer. This moment comes immediately after his first good drive.

—P. G. Wodehouse

I regard the drive as the game's Big Shot. You can talk all you like about putting and chipping, and this shot and that one. But if you can't put the ball out there in playing position, all the rest of the words can be sung to the tune of "Somewhere Over the Rainbow."

—Tony Lema

A driver is the key to the golf round—the key that starts your car, the key that opens your house.

—Lee Trevino

Driving

Back in the old days, they didn't call it a driver. They referred to it as a "play club." In other words, it was the club you used to put the ball in play—maybe *keep* the ball in play. If you feel like you're just trying to get the ball into play, it's easier to avoid that urge to swing too hard.

—*Neal Lancaster*

Always—and I mean ALWAYS—tee the ball on par-3 holes, or any other time you play your opening shot with an iron.

—*Jack Nicklaus*

A curious thing I have noticed about golf is that a festering grievance sometimes does wonders for a man's drive.

—*P. G. Wodehouse*

When the average golfer takes out his driver he calls for all our faith, when he tees up the ball he calls for all our hope, and when he drives, for all our charity.

—*Ted Osborne*

The stories of bad scores rarely start
with, "I ripped one down the middle."

—*Colin Montgomerie*

I always tried to remind myself of the great number of
times I would follow a sequence of bad shots with a
good one—or even a great one. As long as this was a
possibility, I reasoned, then why not *expect* good ones to
follow bad ones—especially off the tee, where you can
recover with good iron shots, chips, or putts and still
have a good hole?

—*Sam Snead*

The biggest disaster shots in the game
are usually tee shots.

—*Raymond Floyd*

If I were you, I would give your driver to
your worst enemy.

—*John Jacobs*

It's no accident that some of the best drivers in the game
have used the fade as their bread-and-butter shot. Sam
Snead, Ben Hogan, Jack Nicklaus, and Lee Trevino, just

to name a few, are among the most accurate drivers in history, and all are notorious for fading the ball when they *had* to hit the fairway.

—*Corey Pavin*

Golf is like tennis. The game doesn't start until the serve gets in.

—*Peter Thomson*

The shots that stick in my mind are not drives, but the approaches, recoveries, and putts. . . . Don't misunderstand me, I regard the driver as the most important club in the bag. But distance is usually much less of a factor in my mind than giving myself the best position for the ensuing shot.

—*Jack Nicklaus*

SECTION 4

Golf Is a Two-Handed Game

SETUP, ALIGNMENT, AND GRIP

Most of the things that contribute to a bad shot in golf occur before you begin your backswing.

—Jim Flick

Correct alignment is *not* like riding a bicycle. You can forget. You can slip into bad habits.

—Jim Flick

The basic factor in all good golf is the grip. Get it right, and all other progress follows.

—Tommy Armour

Much is made of how to aim. Take your stance and hold a clubshaft along the front of your thighs. Look where the club is pointing, and you will see where you are aimed. Laying a club on the ground at your feet will tell you very little.

—Harvey Penick

Setup, Alignment, and Grip

If you haven't had any instruction, it's almost certain that the first things you presently position are your feet, plonking them down in what you hope are the right locations, followed by the clubhead. Break that habit as fast as you can. Because you must align everything else relative to where it faces, always—repeat, always—aim the clubhead first.

—John Jacobs

If on certain holes you go out of bounds or into water or rough so much you think you are jinxed, why don't you try checking your stance? Place the club at the tips of your toes and often you'll be amazed to learn that you actually are aiming at trouble.

—Tommy Armour

A routine is not a routine if you have to think about it.

—Davis Love, Jr.

You can fake about anything, but a bad grip will follow you to the grave.

—Gary McCord

Good golfers are good golfers largely because they have learned and *accepted* that, no matter how fine the gun's firing action, unless it is aimed correctly it won't deliver the missile to the target. Lesser golfers are so impatient to pull the trigger, or so wrapped up in the mechanics of the swing, that they never master what must come before.

—John Jacobs

You get rewarded at the bottom of the club by what you do at the top end.

—Jerry Barber

When you look down at your grip and see wrinkles in your wrists, chances are you are reaching for the ball and not using the club the way it was designed.

—Tommy Armour

Every golfer has one ideal ball position in his stance. Take a swing without a ball, and take a divot. The beginning of the divot indicates where the ball should be positioned.

—Davis Love, Jr.

The only time your hands should be to the right of the ball at address is when you are addressing a teed-up drive that you will catch on the upswing. Your hands should be ahead of the ball at address for all other shots because you are going to hit those shots on the downswing.

—Tommy Armour

Too many people, I believe, feel so uncomfortable and off balance at address that it's almost impossible for them to get the swing started, let alone finish it.

—Mickey Wright

I have the feeling when I'm taking my stance that someone has just pulled a chair from behind me and I'm waiting for him to put it back.

—Arnold Palmer

SWING: THE ELEMENTS

The hips initiate the downswing. They are the pivotal element in the chain reaction. Starting them first and moving them correctly—this one action practically *makes* the downswing.

—*Ben Hogan*

I can't think of anything worse to try to do with a golf club in your hands than "accelerate and follow through." Does the swing accelerate? Yes. What's making it accelerate? Gravity. . . . Is there a follow-through? Of course there is. Why? Because of the swing, because of momentum. . . . If you think "accelerate and follow through" when you swing, then you are going to try to help momentum. Believe me, momentum doesn't need any help.

—*Martin Hall*

A great many players turn their shoulders and think that their hip action is correct. What they don't realize is that you can turn the shoulders while keeping the hips fixed, but when you turn the hips, the shoulders go along.

—*Tommy Armour*

Quiet hands respond on their own to the weight of the clubhead. Tight hands have to be told what to do.

—*Jim Flick*

Swing: The Elements

It is very rare that tension is observed in a practice swing, and this is so because the player, not feeling the necessity of being entirely correct, comes closer to assuming a natural posture. Let him take this naturalness into the actual shot; let him simplify his preliminary motions as much as possible; and let him start the ball on its way without hurry.

—Bobby Jones

The sooner you understand that you swing the clubhead with your hands, that from this cause comes automatically the effect of making all the correct body movements, the nearer you will be to the perfect swing. And perfection is achieved not when there is no longer anything to add, but when there is no longer anything to take away.

—Ernest Jones

Whatever amount of controlled turn you can make while feeling as if you have something in reserve is the right length of backswing for you.

—Butch Harmon

No one pays enough attention to just how much we play by sound. . . . I try to make even beginners aware of it, how important it is to listen and feel. Try to hit the ball squarely, listen, then try to reproduce that sound. The more you hear it, the better you're going to swing it.

—*Gloria Armstrong*

"Keep your left arm straight" is a myth. It's more important to keep your muscles free from tension. Loose muscles let you make a bigger turn and swing the club faster.

—*Gale Peterson*

The majority of players hit their iron shots badly because they are afraid of hitting down. . . . These players keep their weight back on the right leg and try to scoop the ball up. That's the cause of most topped iron shots and plowing up the turf before the ball is hit.

—*Tommy Armour*

Do not use your body to move the club. Let your body *respond* to the moving of the club.

—*Jim Flick*

The cardinal principle of all golf shot-making is that if you move your head, you ruin body action.

—*Tommy Armour*

Swing: The Elements

Head-lifting is caused by fear and anxiety. You are seeking the result before you have struck the ball. You did not trust your swing.

—Ernest Jones

> I never did see the sense in keeping my head down. The only reason I play golf is to see where the ball goes.
>
> *—Charles Price*

The waggle gives the golfer a running start. It blends right into the swing. For all general points and purposes, the backswing is simply an extension of the way the golfer takes the club back on the waggle.

—Ben Hogan

> The good player swings through the ball while the awkward player hits at it.
>
> *—Ken Venturi*

The shorter the club, the shorter the backswing, the shorter the follow-through. There's no need to drop the wedge down your back at the completion of the swing, as you might the driver. Let the club stop at whatever point in the follow-through it runs out of momentum.

—Jack Nicklaus

Whether you are playing a full driver or a five-iron or a wedge, you make no conscious variation in the way you perform your swing. Without your knowing it, your swing will change slightly as the length of the shaft of the club changes.

—Ben Hogan

There is some psychological mystery about the rushing at the top of the swing I've never been able to solve. The ball is going to stay just where it is until it is hit, so there's no valid reason for making a mad dash at it.

—Tommy Armour

It is an invariable rule that if you start the arms first—either at the beginning or at the top of the swing—the result is bad.

—Harry Vardon

A hit must be perfectly timed, but a swing will time itself.

—Grantland Rice

SWING: THE ESSENCE

Understand that golf is neither a right-handed nor a left-handed game, but a two-handed one.

—Ernest Jones

Instead of trying to maneuver the ball with your body, arms, and hands, trust your swing and the club you select for the shot.

—Ben Hogan

Golf is an art form, not a science. You don't have to conform to some mechanical model of a perfect swing. You just have to remember your goal—to have a bunch of fun by making a little white ball go from the ground here in front of you into a target area over there.

—Jim Flick

The flight of the ball ALWAYS tells you EVERYTHING you need to know to become a better player.

—John Jacobs

"My swing is too fast" may be the biggest misconception ever. Think about it. If you take a fast, lousy swing and slow it down, all you've got left is a slow, lousy swing. Most people swing too slow, not too fast.

—*Hank Haney*

We all have particular quirks and faults in our golf swing we wish were not there. We anguish over how to make them go away. But they never do and they never will. It's all part of our "thumb print." Don't forsake your thumb print. It is who you are. Work with it, not against it.

—*Roger Maltbie*

The golf swing is like sex. You can't be thinking about the mechanics of the act while you're performing.

—*Dave Hill*

Nobody ever swung a club too slowly.

—*Bobby Jones*

Everyone's becoming so swing conscious you need to be careful. Attention needs to be brought back to basics. The swing, the swing, the swing—well, it's like a simple piece of furniture. A chair. Nothing more. Is the chair solid? Will it hold you? Will it stand up over time? Good. Then sit in it. Appreciate the wood, the feel. Then do what we most often do with a chair: Forget it's there.

—*Shirley Englehorn*

The point is that it doesn't matter if you look like a beast before or after the hit, as long as you look like a beauty at the moment of impact.

—*Seve Ballesteros*

There is only one categorical imperative in golf, and that is to hit the ball. There are no minor absolutes.

—*Sir Walter Simpson*

TEMPO, TIMING, AND RHYTHM

If by nature you do things quickly, or slowly, you're going to swing the golf club basically the same way. Forcing yourself to an opposite extreme is rarely going to work because it's too contrary to your basic instincts or impulses—especially when you are under competitive pressure.

—Jack Nicklaus

All swings have one thing in common: whatever the tempo, the speeds of the backswing and downswing are the same.

—Johnny Miller

The common denominator for all golfers is tempo, so I advise every golfer, no matter their skill level, to think tempo—the smooth transition from backswing to downswing—as the primary swing thought.

—Hale Irwin

Above all, tempo is the great equalizer. It compensates for mechanical flaws in your swing, and will reduce your slices, hooks, and inconsistent contact.

—Bill Moretti

When you stroke with timing and rhythm, the ball sails straight down the fairway, and for distance. *It is effortless power, not powerful effort.*

—Ernest Jones

Tempo, Timing, and Rhythm

Everyone who knows me knows I love music. I used my music to help me maintain my swing's rhythm. For me, waltz time, or 3/4 time, was perfect for the correct golf swing tempo.

—Sam Snead

Swing like you were being paid by the hour, not the job.

—Davis Love, Jr.

Rhythm is best expressed in any swing directed at a cigar stump or a dandelion head.

—Grantland Rice

You can't take a car from a dead start and put it immediately up to 70 miles an hour. No matter how powerful your engine, you must have a gradual acceleration of speed. So it is in a golf swing.

—Mickey Wright

There is a blood relationship between waggle and tempo. Show me someone who has a quick, short waggle and I will

show you someone who has a quick, short
swing. Show me a long, languid waggle,
and I'll show you a person who has got a
long, flowing swing.

—*Roger Maltbie*

The most important single move in establishing your
tempo and rhythm is your takeaway. It sets the beat for
everything that comes later. Strive on every shot to move
the club back as *deliberately* as possible, consistent with
swinging it [back] rather than taking it [back].

—*Jack Nicklaus*

One very simple tip will infinitely improve the timing of
most golfers. Merely pause briefly at the top of the backswing.

—*Tommy Armour*

A very fine [drill] for improving your tempo, smoothing
out your rhythm, and improving your balance is to swing
with your feet together, I mean actually touching. . . . This
[practice] is a fine way to develop a tempo slower than the
one you've been playing with.

—*Jack Nicklaus*

Golf is a game of motion and rhythm, not position and mechanics.

—*Martin Hall*

I want to swing aggressively. But I don't want to look like I am.

—*Brian Watts*

POWER

You will hit the ball farther more frequently when you don't try to hit it far.

—*Sam Snead*

There are really two ways of increasing your distance. You can learn to swing the clubhead faster. Or you can learn to deliver it to the ball more accurately.

—*Jack Nicklaus*

AS HOGAN SAID . . .

My first rule is, "Distance without direction is worse than no distance at all."

—*Nancy Lopez*

To hit the ball farther, think of creating your maximum clubhead speed past the ball—not at it, and certainly not before it.

—*Randy Smith*

No power on earth will deter men from using a ball that will add to the length of their drive.

—*Golf Illustrated, 1902*

Many shots are spoiled at the last instant by efforts to add a few more yards. This impedes, rather than aids the stroke.

—*Bobby Jones*

Golf is a game to be played with two hands. Your left hand guides the club and keeps the face in the desired position for the hit, and power pours through the right hand and the club. Whack the hell out of the ball with the right hand.

—*Tommy Armour*

Power

The hands are the key to transmitting power from the body to the club. The club shaft is held more in the fingers than the palms of your hands. In the palm, it is impossible to get any zip into the shot.

—Sam Snead

Have you ever noticed that your longest shots are also your straightest shots?

—Ken Venturi

You should *want* to hit the ball as far as you can; don't be ashamed of that.

—Davis Love, Jr.

About the only positive contribution of uncontrolled pursuit of power is to make golf ball and equipment manufacturers rich.

—Jim Flick

SECTION 5

Hope for the Best,
Expect the Worst,
and Take What Comes Along

WARMING UP

The man who runs from his office to the golf club, gulps a sandwich, belches and races to the first tee has no business howling in anguish when he puts his first two shots in the woods, then tops a 3-iron shot into the pond.

—Tony Lema

When warming up before a round, make the last shot you hit on the practice tee the same as the first shot you have to hit on the course.

—Ken Venturi

If you arrive at the course with just a few minutes to warm up before a round, use that time to hit chip shots. The chip shot, being a short version of the full swing, tells your muscles and your golfing brain to get ready to play.

—Harvey Penick

The part shot from 50 to 60 yards out is golf's "money shot." When warming up before playing, always devote time to 60-yard shots, even if that's all you do.

—Jim Flick

Warming Up

When I begin my pre-round warm-up routine, I'm usually looking to establish my rhythm and tempo for the day. I'm trying to get those muscles loose and get a feel for my motion that day and how fast or slow things are moving and maybe get a grip on my timing. That's all I do for the first twenty-five balls or so because, as all golfers know, you feel different every day.

—*Ben Crenshaw*

FIRST TEE

On the first tee, a golfer must expect only two things of himself: to have fun, and to focus his mind properly on every shot.

—*Bob Rotella*

If one has not learned enough of golf by the time he steps onto the first tee, then he has run out of time.

—*Bobby Jones*

The test of a great golfer is his ability to recover from a bad start.

—*P. G. Wodehouse*

Most amateurs on the first tee rush themselves. Because they feel anxious, especially when there are a lot of people watching, they want to get things over with. They pull out the driver, tee it up without collecting themselves, and give it a hit-it-and-hope whack.

—*Raymond Floyd*

A veteran player of my acquaintance tells me that he has for many years approached the first tee with one firm resolution—to take it easy for the first three holes; not to expect too much, but rather to feel that he is likely to hit a few bad shots until he finally begins to get the feel of the thing.

—*Ernest Jones*

TROUBLE

Golf is the game that evolved over humps, hollows, sand craters, ridges, dikes, and clumps of heather and gorse. These features made up a game that is a trial of luck and ingenuity. How dull to have no obstacles to dodge or need no "escape" shots in one's repertoire.

—*Peter Thomson*

Trouble

The primary reason players often make spectacular trouble shots, causing the ball to go under, around, and over obstacles, is that *they work harder on visualizing these shots* than on those from less demanding positions.

—*Gary Wiren*

When I hit a shot into trouble, I expect the worst. . . . When I get there and find that I can actually hit the ball—which you usually can—it changes my mood for the better right away.

—*Corey Pavin*

On the course, what is feared is like a magnet. Water, bunkers, trees, ravines, high grass—whatever you fear turns magnetic.

—*Wiffi Smith*

Don't let the bad shots get to you. Don't let yourself become angry. The true scramblers are thick-skinned. And they always beat the whiners.

—*Paul Runyan*

Amateur golf is a game of trouble shots and one-putt pars. It follows therefore that good scrambling is the amateur's fastest, most direct route to better golf.

—*George Peper*

Making a par after chipping out of the trees can destroy an opponent. Taking a double or triple bogey after hacking your way out of the woods can destroy you.

—*Francisco Lopez*

With either a downhill lie or an uphill lie, always play the ball nearer the higher foot.

—*Jackie Burke, Jr.*

When it's breezy, hit it easy.

—*Davis Love, Jr.*

If you are in the woods, don't act like a seamstress. Your job is not to thread needles but to get the ball back into the fairway.

—*Arnold Palmer*

Be prepared to get it up and down on the first hole. That way, you always expect the unexpected and you're ready for anything.

—*Jackie Burke, Jr.*

ROUGH

Obviously, the prime objective in playing from rough is to minimize the club's contact with it. Equally obviously, an upright swing achieves that objective better than a flat swing, because of the sharper angle at which the clubhead rises from and returns to the ball. Keep that in mind every time you enter the tall grass.

—Jack Nicklaus

A rough should have high grass. When you go bowling they don't give you anything for landing in the gutter, do they?

—Lee Trevino

If rough is growing in the direction of the shot, the ball will come out easier and faster; if it is against that direction, the grass will resist the club, so *you must swing harder.*

—Raymond Floyd

The secret in the rough is to take a few dozen practice swings with a 2-iron (a scythe is good, too).

—Tom Callahan

Test the rough with a practice swing to
determine how much resistance it will
offer to your swing.

—*Byron Nelson*

When the average golfer goes into rough, too often he
gets up to his ball and the first question he asks himself is,
"What club do I need to reach the green?" That is putting
the cart before the horse, in my book. Sure the distance is
one factor, but the first thing to look at is your lie. It's no
good fingering a wood when you have a sand wedge lie
on your hands. The lie you have in most instances dictates
the type of shot you have to hit.

—*Johnny Miller*

WATER

The difference between a sand trap and water is the difference between a car crash and an airplane crash. You
have a chance of recovering from a car crash.

—*Bobby Jones*

Water

Only bullfighting and the water hole are left as vestigial evidence of what a bloody savage man used to be. Only in golf is this sort of contrived swindle allowed.

—Tommy Bolt

The best advice I can offer for playing a
ball out of water is—don't.
—Tony Lema

A good way to block out water fronting a green is to focus on a noticeable feature behind it, such as the edge of a bunker, a tree, or a mound, and play to a distance on the rear of the green.

—Robert Trent Jones, Jr.

When your shot has to carry over a water hazard, you can either hit one more club or two more balls.

—Henry Beard

From the roaring oceans to the majestic lakes, the rushing streams and quiet ponds and burns, water adds a test to golf that entrances.

—Robert Trent Jones

The average player plays an old ball at a water hole. . . .
The instant the fellow picks out the old ball and tees it he
is licked, psychologically. He is saying to himself, subconsciously, "I'm going to fluff this one into the water."

—Tommy Armour

Being a Scotsman, I am naturally opposed to water in its
undiluted state.

—Dr. Alister Mackenzie

SECTION 6

*Keep Your Head Up,
and in the Game*

COURSE MANAGEMENT

You can hit your shots great and still shoot 80 every day because of poor management. The shots are 30 percent of the game. Judgment is 70 percent.

—Ben Hogan

I believe the lay-up second shot is one of the most overlooked in golf. When I think of good lay-up players, I think of Tom Kite. . . . He pays close attention to his second shot on a par 5 so he leaves himself perfect sandwedge distance from which he is deadly accurate.

—Corey Pavin

Even before you step up to the ball, have
a full battle plan for the hole worked out.

—Arnold Palmer

Take a club that you can swing at 80 percent and still get to the hole. Conserve your energy; you have a long life ahead of you!

—Gary McCord

Course Management

> It *sometimes* makes sense to play aggres-
> sively, but it always makes good sense to
> play smart.
>
> —*Jim Flick*

Most amateurs don't take enough club. They presume
they'll hit every shot perfectly and make their club selec-
tions based on the maximum distance, instead of the average distance, they hit each club. As a result, any shot that
isn't flushed comes up short.

> —*Robert Baker*

In my experience, the higher the handicap, the more dar-
ing the player. I see golfers who don't break 100 trying to
play shots a tour pro wouldn't touch. . . . Don't let that
rare success on a risky shot determine your thinking; your
overall past performance is a much better yardstick.

> —*Craig Bunker*

Some days you're on the range, and it hooks or slices, and
you go out on the course, it hooks or slices. So let it hook
or slice, don't try to fix it once you're in the game. Score
with what you've got that day.

> —*Gloria Armstrong*

The important question is not how good
your good shots are—it's how bad are
your bad ones?

—Harvey Penick

It's Old Man Par and you, match or medal. And Old Man Par
is a patient soul, who never shoots a birdie and never incurs a
buzzard. He's a patient soul, Old Man Par. And if you would
travel the long route with him, you must be patient, too.

—Bobby Jones

Hit the shot you know you can hit, not
the one you think you should.

—Bob Rotella

Jack Nicklaus played his entire career by hitting mostly to the
center of the green. . . . Amateurs go flag hunting a lot too often, and it severely hurts their scoring ability and enjoyment.

—Jim McLean

Like pool, golf is primarily a game of position. The professional pool player never takes one shot at a time. He or-
ganizes a series of shots in his mind in order to sink all of

the balls on the table. The key is to get a good "leave," or an ideal position for the next shot.

—*Robert Trent Jones, Jr.*

Golf is not a game you can rush. For every stroke you try to force out of her, she is going to extract two in return.

—*Dave Hill*

Hit the ball up to the hole. . . . You meet a better class of people up there.

—*Ben Hogan*

Never aim where a dead-straight shot will kill you.

—*Jim McLean*

If you don't know the [exact] distances you hit your clubs—and most golfers don't—then you're giving away a lot of shots on the course.

—*Gary Wiren*

When laying up, lay up.

—*Jim McLean*

Percentage golf is not so much the science of playing the game with the shots of which you are capable as it is of playing without the shots of which you are incapable.

—Jackie Burke, Jr.

Every golfer should establish his own par on a hole and play for that par.

—H. H. Ramsay

Play the game, strategically, from the green back to the tee. Design every shot for the easiest putt possible.

—Jackie Burke, Jr.

Play the shot that makes the next shot easy.

—Tommy Armour

ARCHITECTURE

While there are critics who believe my courses are too difficult, the ardent golfer would play Mount Everest if somebody put a flagstick on top.

—Pete Dye

Architecture

Every golfer worthy of the name should have some acquaintance with the principles of golf course design, not only for the betterment of the game, but for his own selfish enjoyment. Let him know a good hole from a bad one and the reasons for a bunker here and another there, and he will be a long way towards pulling his score down to respectable limits. When he has taught himself to study a hole from the point of view of the man who laid it out, he will be much more likely to play it correctly.

—Bobby Jones

Comparatively few golfers ever show that they are aware that the golf architect tries to design a course that rewards an intelligent golfer and penalizes a stupid one.

—Tommy Armour

A good golf course is like good music or good anything else. It is not necessarily a course which appeals the first time one plays it, but one which grows on the player the more frequently they visit it.

—Dr. Alister Mackenzie

A golf course is a field of maneuver and action, employing the military and engineering side of the game. It opens up a series of tactical and strategical opportunities, the implications of which it would be well for every golfer to grasp. It is important to emphasize the necessity for the golfer to use his head as much as his hands; or to make his mental agility match his physical ability.

—H. N. Wethered and
Tom Simpson

There are two ways of widening the gap between a good shot and a bad one. One is to inflict a severe and immediate punishment upon the bad shot, to place its perpetrator in a bunker or in some other trouble demanding the sacrifice of a stroke in recovery; the other is to reward the good shot by making the second simpler in proportion to the excellence of the drive.

—Bobby Jones

The idea is to mold nature just sufficiently to give the greatest golf possibilities.

—Donald Ross

There is no necessity for artificial barriers. Play does not have to be systematically controlled. An opposite principle is involved. This principle is freedom. And by freedom we compel the golfer to control himself, that is to say, his instincts. . . . If he judges his skill is great enough, he will of his own accord go for a strategic hazard to gain an advantage just as the tennis player will go for the sidelines of the court.

—Max Behr

The strategy of the golf course is the soul of the game. The spirit of golf is to dare a hazard, and by negotiating it reap a reward, while he who fears or declines the issue of the carry, has a longer or harder shot for his second.

—George Thomas

The majority of golfers are agreed that an ideal hole should be a difficult one. . . . It is the successful negotiation of difficulties which gives rise to pleasurable excitement and makes a hole interesting.

—Dr. Alister Mackenzie

The great thing about designing a golf hole is the architect gets to put the spectator or the player at a certain starting point. It is a perfectly controlled perspective, one of the few perfectly controlled perspectives in life. We put down two tee markers and we say, "Stand here, golfer, and nowhere else, and you will look at what we put in front of you."

—Steve Wynn

MENTAL SIDE

It is impossible to outplay an opponent you can't outthink.

—*Lawson Little*

If you could eliminate the occasional bad shot you would be the first person to do so.

—*John Jacobs*

Golf is a game to teach you about the messages from within, about the subtle voices of the body-mind. And once you understand them you can more clearly see your "hamartia," the ways in which your approach to the game reflects your entire life. Nowhere does a man go so naked.

—*Michael Murphy*

I have been able to hope for the best, expect the worst, and take what comes along. If there has been one fundamental reason for my success, this is it.

—*Gene Sarazen*

A man who could retain through his golfing career the almost scornful confidence of the non-player would be unbeatable. Fortunately such an attitude of mind is beyond the scope of human nature.

—*P. G. Wodehouse*

Doubt is the number one cause of missed shots.

—*Davis Love, Jr.*

As for the ideal golf temperament, there isn't enough of it at large to collect for laboratory purposes. Except at the rarest of intervals, it doesn't exist.

—*Grantland Rice*

You can't possibly be a good golfer if you don't think that you are a good golfer. The best that you can perform is to the level of your own expectations, but no better.

—*Francisco Lopez*

If I miss a shot, a drive, an iron shot or whatever it may be, I do not catechize myself as to what I did wrong or wonder if I shall do it wrong again next time; I simply accept the miss as an inevitable result of being a very frail or ordinary mortal.

—*Bernard Darwin*

Everything with its head down gets eaten.

—*Jackie Burke, Jr.*

Take responsibility for your own ball and your own score—the only things you have control over.

—*Sam Snead*

It's OK to have butterflies. Just get them flying in formation.

—*Francisco Lopez*

There's a wonderful Japanese phrase I like to use that says, "A bridge was not built to take its life's load all in one day." What we often try to do is pack the needs of a whole round into a very small set of circumstances. "On this hole maybe I can. . . . I really need a. . . . Next hole I gotta. . . . Then maybe. . . ." I needa, I gotta, I needa—well, the Needas and the Gottas can't play golf. They self-destruct. Remember this: A single bridge. A moment's load. Here and now.

—*Annette Thompson*

Let your attitude determine your golf game. Don't let your golf game determine your attitude.

—*Davis Love, Jr.*

Mental Side

The question is: Which comes first, enjoying the game or playing it well? I believe the golfer who drives into the parking lot anticipating a good time can't help but play well most of the time. There's something to be said for optimism and a carefree spirit.

—Corey Pavin

We can, if we wish, pretend to enjoy the shots which frighten us. We can positively make ourselves look forward to playing as many of them as possible. Instead of fearing them we can stimulate an interest in them. A delicate pitch over a bunker can be converted by a little judicious mental effort into a delightful adventure.

—Joyce Wethered

Missing a short putt does not mean you have to hit your next drive out of bounds.

—Henry Cotton

Learn to bear your ill fortune without appealing for sympathy.

—Harold H. Hilton

The shopworn admonition to forget the last shot and play the one in hand was meant to apply as much to the good ones as to the bad. It is just as important to forget the 3's as the 6's.

—*Bobby Jones*

If profanity had an influence on the flight
of the ball, the game would be played far
better than it is.

—*Horace Hutchinson*

There is no such thing as a golfer playing over his head. A hot streak is simply a glimpse of a golfer's true potential.

—*Bob Rotella*

Take it from me—the Tour pros couldn't care less what the other players in their threesome are hitting. To them, the various clubs are like surgical tools to a surgeon. The numbers on the clubs simply represent an angle of clubface loft on each of those "tools"—and they are only interested in using the tool they can swing in a controlled fashion, in order to drop the ball next to the cup. Start thinking this way right now and leave all the crowing about reaching the 14th with a drive and a wedge to others.

—*Butch Harmon*

Mental Side

I've never played a perfect 18 holes. There is no such thing. I expect to make at least seven mistakes a round. Therefore, when I make a bad shot, I don't worry about it. It's just one of the seven.

—Walter Hagen

I've never missed a putt in my mind.

—Jack Nicklaus

If you dub a shot, don't berate yourself unduly. Golf is supposed to cure ulcers, not create them.

—Arnold Palmer

Nobody thinks the way they should on every shot, nobody's that good. You were born human.

—Tom Kite

It's not the walking or the swinging that tires you at golf; it's the thinking or, more often, the ineffectual effort of trying to think and not knowing how to do it that wears you down.

—Tommy Armour

Learn how to quarantine the bad part of your game in order to keep it from infecting the rest of your game. If your approach shots seem to be turning sour, look to your driving and putting to carry the load until your short irons start working again.

—*Arnold Palmer*

Hitting a golf ball is an act so precise that there is unlimited room for error. That error begins in the mind and finds expression in the swing.

—*Lorne Rubenstein*

The most important shot in golf is the next one.

—*Ben Hogan*

MATCH PLAY

Golf matches are not won on the fairways or greens. They are won on the tee—the first tee.

—*Anonymous*

I play golf with friends, but we don't play friendly golf.

—*Ben Hogan*

Match Play

People say, "Play the course; don't play the man," but I never believed that. Especially in match play, you have to keep one eye on your opponent.

—*Sam Snead*

I hear players say they want to hit first to put the pressure on. Not me. I'd rather hit second in match play no matter what my opponent does. I want all the information possible so I know what I have to do. If my opponent hits a terrific shot, I know I have to hit a terrific shot. If he gets in trouble, my options change.

—*Tom Watson*

When you are playing for five bucks and you've got two bucks in your pocket—that's pressure.

—*Lee Trevino*

If your adversary is badly bunkered, there is no rule against your standing over him and counting his strokes aloud, with increasing gusto as their number mounts up; but it will be a wise precaution to arm yourself with a niblick before doing so, so as to meet him on even terms.

—*Horace Hutchinson*

Bets lengthen putts and shorten drives.

—*Henry Beard*

There is nothing more wearing to a leader who is playing well than the knowledge that his enemy is refusing to crack. If by hanging on we can drive that knowledge into him, we may make him crack instead and that crack will be a bad one when it comes.

—*Bernard Darwin*

If your adversary is a hole or two down, there is no serious cause for alarm in his complaining of a severely sprained wrist, or an acute pain, resembling lumbago, which checks his swing. Should he happen to win the next hole, these symptoms will in all probability become less troublesome.

—*Horace Hutchinson*

No matter what happens—*never give up on a hole.* . . . In tossing in your cards after a bad beginning you also undermine your whole game, because to quit between tee and green is more habit-forming than drinking a highball before breakfast.

—*Sam Snead*

Match Play

Not paying [a golf debt] is like ordering dinner, eating the damn thing and then not expecting to pay for it.

—Doug Sanders

This is really the whole secret of good match play—simply to play your best and steadiest, and not to care about the opponent's game until it is absolutely necessary to do so.

—James Braid

The muttered hint, "Remember, you have a stroke here," freezes my joints like a blast from Siberia.

—John Updike

Think like the underdog. The underdog always has the advantage. . . . The favorite, meanwhile, is prone to negativism, worrying about how embarrassing it would be to lose.

—Dr. Bob Rotella

However unlucky you may be, it really is not fair to expect your adversary's grief for your undeserved misfortunes to be as poignant as your own.

—Horace Hutchinson

Remember that you do not so often win holes as the result of your own brilliant play as by the mistakes that the other man makes.

—James Braid

I never learned anything from a match that I won.

—Bobby Jones

Don't be afraid of the player with a good grip and a bad swing. Don't be afraid of a player with a bad grip and a good swing. The player to beware of is the one with the bad grip and the bad swing. If he's reached your level, he has grooved his faults and knows how to score.

—Harvey Penick

When making a match, do not try to get a greater allowance of strokes than that to which you are entitled on your handicap, alleging to your opponent that the said handicap is an unfair one. Your opponent may think you are a little too "keen"; and if he grants your improper request, and you should then win the match, he may think some other things besides.

—Harry Vardon

RULES AND ETIQUETTE

If there's one thing golf demands above
all else, it's honesty.

—Jack Nicklaus

Every golfer is on his honor.

—Donald Ross

Watch your opponent's (or partner's) ball and mark the
spot carefully if it should land in trouble. . . . It is a great
comfort to know that those with you will extend the same
courtesy to you.

—Peter Dobereiner

This is my attitude toward my favorite game. I have its
honor to support. So has each one who enters its fold. An
error in count, an error that moves the ball, an error that in
any way makes you take improper advantage over your
opponent, seen or unseen, is the worst error in the whole
game. We begin with the question, who has the honor?

—Glenna Collett Vare

Don't get into the habit of playing "winter rules." If you do, you'll never learn to play the shots you need to be a decent golfer. Winter rules are generally an amusing delusion. They aid neither in the development of the turf nor of the player.

—*Tommy Armour*

Nonchalant putts count the same as chalant putts.

—*Henry Beard*

If the average American player would only realize how much easier it is to play well when he is swinging along at a good rate, he would surely gird up his loins and walk a little faster.

—*H. J. Whigham*

Some golfers seem to have no genius for figures. They cannot count correctly and, unfortunately, their general tendency is to be one stroke shy rather than one too many.

—*Jerome Travers*

Rules and Etiquette

You have a perfect right to ask a golfer to hole out every single putt; and no golfer ought to take offense at your so asking him.

—Horace Hutchinson

A man who gets into a rage, swears, and breaks his clubs, and petulantly drives his ball off into the woods should either reform or give up the game. . . . Let him go beat carpets! No true lover of golf will mourn his loss!

—Jerome Travers

> There is no surer nor [more] painful way to learn a rule than to be penalized for breaking it.
>
> *—Tom Watson*

The first thing you should do when you see that your ball has settled in a divot is to tell yourself that it's a bad break, that it happens to everyone, and that you really have to concentrate on this shot. . . . Oh, and you might also resolve never to leave a divot unrepaired yourself.

—Ken Venturi

It would be an insult to your good taste and intelligence to tell you how to behave on the links, because it is only necessary to remember that for the time being the golf course is your garden and the clubhouse is your temporary home.

—Henry Cotton

If golfers keep on playing so slowly, on the green particularly, one way to correct the situation is to knock the ball into them. There will be a short delay while you have a hell of a fight, but from then on you'll move faster.

—Horace Hutchinson

The man who can go into a patch of rough alone, with the knowledge that only God is watching him, and play his ball where it lies is the man who will serve you faithfully and well.

—P. G. Wodehouse

SECTION 7

*If You Can Walk,
You Can Play*

GETTING OLDER

Certainly the older golfer can't hit the ball as far as the young, flat-bellied player. But once you reach the fringe of the green, you and the younger player become no worse than equals. And you can even have the advantage if you are faithful in practicing your short game.

—Harvey Penick

Attitude is the one place an older golfer has an advantage. By age fifty, a golfer has perspective and wisdom that should give him a formidable mental game.

—Raymond Floyd

Anyone who says he plays better at 55 than he did at 25 wasn't very good at 25.

—Bob Brue

What you always have to remember is that golf is a game that you can play almost forever. In other sports, a 40-year-old athlete is an old man.

—Curtis Strange

Getting Older

The golfer is never old until he is decrepit. So long as providence allows him the use of two legs active enough to carry him around the green, and two arms supple enough to take a "half-swing," there is no reason why his enjoyment in the game need be seriously diminished. Decay no doubt there is; long driving has gone forever; and something less of firmness and accuracy may be noted even in the short game. But the decay has come by such slow graduations, it has delayed so long and spared so much, that it is robbed of half its bitterness.

—Lord Balfour

You don't want to fiddle around too much with a swing that has been useful to you for decades, but now is the time to add a 5- or 6-wood and especially a 7-wood to your bag. Seasoned Citizens get their loft from their clubs, not from their swing. Adding loft is a reliable substitute for youth and strength.

—Harvey Penick

Competitiveness is a personality thing and competitive people don't become pushovers the day they turn 50.

—Hale Irwin

Golfers who have the yips usually are older rather than younger. The reason isn't age itself or the loss of nerves, however. It's simply that a golfer usually has to have played for a long time, endured poor mechanics, and many missed putts before that fear of missing becomes so great it takes hold in the mind. The yips don't happen overnight. It takes many years of bad practice before they take over, thus the tendency for older golfers to develop them.

—Dave Pelz

Those clubs don't know how old you are.

—Claudia Trevino

You're never too old to play golf. If you can walk, you can play.

—Louise Suggs

List of Sources

A History of Golf. Browning, Robert. 26, 27, 34.

A Round of Golf with Tommy Armour. Armour, Tommy. 18, 19, 94, 101, 109.

Advanced Golf. Braid, James. 28, 45, 54, 113, 14.

The American Golfer (magazine). 16, 61, 100, 102, 105.

The Architectural Side of Golf. Wethered, Joyce and Simpson, Tom. 101.

The Art of Golf. Simpson, Sir Walter. 19, 24, 41, 42, 43, 45, 77.

The Badminton Library: Golf. Hutchinson, Horace. 117.

Break 100 Now! Adams, Michael and Tomasi, Dr. T. J. 31.

Bury Me in a Pot Bunker. Dye, Peter. 100.

Champagne Tony's Golf Tips. Lema, Tony. 36, 60, 86, 93.

Classic Golf Tips by Tommy Armour. Armour, Tommy. 67, 68, 69.

Classic Instruction. Jones, Robert and Crenshaw, Ben. 41, 51, 54.

Clubsmarts. Abrahams, Jonathan. 27.

The Common Sense of Golf. Whigham, H. J. 116.

The Complete Golfer. Vardon, Harry. 16, 114.

Court Hustler. Riggs, Bobby. 110.

Different Strokes. Vold, Mona. 17, 72, 76, 89, 97, 106.

The Dogged Victims of Inexorable Fate. Jenkins, Dan. 18, 43.

Down the Fairway. Keeler, O. B. and Jones, Robert. 45, 46, 98, 114.

The Duffer's Handbook of Golf. Rice, Grantland et al. 18, 29, 35, 79, 105.

List of Sources

The Education of a Golfer. Snead, Sam. 112.

The Elements of Scoring. Floyd, Raymond. 45, 47, 62, 88, 120.

Every Shot I Take. Love, Davis III. 33, 37, 45, 52, 67, 68, 79, 83, 90, 105, 106.

Fairways and Greens. Jenkins, Dan. 19.

Five Lessons. Hogan, Ben. 69, 73, 74.

Jim Flick on Golf. Flick, Jim. 38, 48, 66, 70, 72, 74, 75, 81, 83, 86, 97.

The Four Cornerstones of Winning Golf. Harmon, Claude, Jr. 71, 108.

From 60 Yards In. Floyd, Raymond. 91.

The Game for a Lifetime. Penick, Harvey. 34, 46.

The Game I Love. Snead, Sam. 55, 62, 79, 106.

Getting Up and Down. Watson, Tom. 23, 38, 40, 52.

The Gist of Golf. Vardon, Harry. 74.

Golf. Cotton, Henry. 32, 34, 118, 120.

Golf, The Greatest Game. The United States Golf Association. 102, 109.

Golf: The Lore of the Links. Celsi, Teresa. 104.

Golf: The Money Swing. Vare, Ned. 22.

Golf à la *Carte.* Dobereiner, Peter. 47, 115.

Golf Architecture. Mackenzie, Dr. Alister. 101, 103.

Golf Architecture in America. Thomas, George. 103.

Golf Begins at 50. Player, Gary. 35.

Golf Begins at Forty. Snead, Sam. 81.

Golf by Design. Jones, Robert Trent, Jr. 93, 98.

Golf Digest (magazine). 16, 17, 22, 27, 29, 30, 42, 56, 57, 59, 62, 67, 72, 78, 81, 82, 83, 89, 91, 92, 109, 111, 113, 120, 122.

Golf Doctor. Jacobs, John. 59.

List of Sources

Golf Doctor. Middlecoff, Dr. Cary. 51.

Golf for Dummies. McCord, Gary. 67, 96.

Golf for Young Players. Vare, Glenna Collett. 115.

Golf Has Never Failed Me. Ross, Donald. 29, 115.

Golf Illustrated (magazine). 82.

Golf in a Nutshell. Jacobs, John. 62, 104.

Golf in the Kingdom. Murphy, Michael. 104.

Golf Is a Very Simple Game. Lopez, Francisco. 90, 105, 106.

Golf Is Not a Game of Perfect. Rotella, Dr. Bob. 87, 108.

Golf Magazine. 32, 46, 50, 90, 97, 106, 120.

Golf Magazine's Complete Book of Golf Instruction. Frank, Jim et al. 41, 48, 49, 53, 69, 78, 79, 82, 88, 89, 107, 112.

Golf Magazine's Course Management Handbook. Wiren, Dr. Gary. 99.

Golf Magazine's Mental Game Handbook. Wiren, Dr. Gary. 89.

Golf My Way. Nicklaus, Jack. 22, 35, 47, 51, 63, 73, 77, 80, 91.

The Golf Omnibus. Wodehouse, P. G. 16, 31, 61, 87, 104.

Golf School. McLean, Jim. 41, 54, 98, 99.

The Golf Swing Simplified. Jacobs, John. 68, 75.

Golf Without Tears. Wodehouse P. G. 17, 25, 60, 118.

Golf World (magazine). 87, 110, 111.

Golf's Little Instruction Book. Witebsky, Arthur. 26, 115.

Golf's Magnificent Challenge. Jones, Robert Trent. 93.

Golfer-at-Large. Price, Charles. 73.

The Golfer's Book of Daily Inspiration. Nelson, Kevin. 35, 98, 111.

Harvey Penick's Little Red Book. Penick, Harvey. 24, 30, 36, 44, 66, 86, 98, 114, 120, 121.

Hints on Golf. Hutchinson, Horace. 24, 108, 111, 112, 113, 118.

List of Sources

Hints on Playing with Steel Shafts. Cotton, Henry. 33.

Hogan. Sampson, Curt. 96, 110.

The Hole Truth. Bolt, Tommy. 28.

How to Break 90/80/Par. McAdams, Cliff. 30.

How to Keep Your Temper on a Golf Course. Bolt, Tommy. 93.

How to Play Golf. Snead, Sam. 83.

How to Play Your Best Golf All the Time. Armour, Tommy. 27, 33, 57, 58, 70, 72, 74, 80, 82, 100, 116.

Inside Sports: Golf. Matuz, Roger. 101.

Bobby Jones' Golf Tips. Jones, Robert. 34.

Bobby Jones on Golf. Jones, Robert. 18, 26, 44, 49, 52, 53, 71, 76, 107.

Ladies' Golf. Hezlet, May. 38.

Learning Golf. Hogan, Chuck. 25.

Bobby Locke on Golf. Locke, Bobby. 44, 58.

The Master of Putting. Low, George. 43.

The Methods of Golf's Masters. Aultman, Dick and Bowden, Ken. 32, 42, 82, 109.

Modern Golf. Hilton, Harold. 107.

Mulligan's Laws. Beard, Henry. 25, 28, 93, 112, 116.

My Million Dollar Shots. Casper, Billy. 48.

My Story. Nicklaus, Jack. 81.

The Mystery of Golf. Haultain, Arnold. 18, 20.

The Natural Way to Better Golf. Burke, Jackie, Jr. 17, 23, 40, 51, 90, 100.

The New York Times (newspaper). 117.

Jack Nicklaus's Lesson Tee. Nicklaus, Jack. 55, 61, 80.

Greg Norman's 100 Instant Golf Lessons. Norman, Greg. 16, 55.

The Only Golf Lesson You'll Ever Need. Haney, Hank. 32, 50, 57, 76

List of Sources

The PGA Manual of Golf. Wiren, Dr. Gary. 31, 33, 35, 36, 40, 47, 63, 66, 68, 73, 77, 110.

The PGA Tour Complete Book of Golf. Corcoran, Michael. 23, 37, 58, 61, 87.

Corey Pavin's Shotmaking. Pavin, Corey. 42, 48, 49, 55, 57, 60, 62, 89, 96, 107.

Play Better Golf. Jacobs, John. 55.

Gary Player's Golf Secrets. Player, Gary. 36.

Practical Golf. Jacobs, John. 47.

Pure Golf. Miller, Johnny. 49, 55, 92.

Putt Like the Pros. Pelz, Dave. 122.

The Quotable Golfer. Windeler, Robert. 92.

Range Rats. Maltbie, Roger. 43, 44, 50, 76, 79, 99.

Situation Golf. Palmer, Arnold. 30, 44, 90, 96, 109, 110.

Smart Golf. Irwin, Hale. 78, 121.

The Snake in the Sandtrap. Trevino, Lee. 60, 122.

Spalding's Golf Guide. Braid, James. 23.

The Spirit of St. Andrews. Mackenzie, Dr. Alister. 94.

Sunday Telegraph (newspaper). 26.

Swing the Clubhead. Jones, Ernest. 71, 73, 75, 78.

Swinging Into Golf. Jones, Ernest. 75, 88.

Teed Off. Hill, Dave. 76, 99.

Thanks for the Game. Cotton, Henry. 28, 107.

Thirty Years of Championship Golf. Sarazen, Gene. 104.

Travers' Golf Book. Travers, Jerome. 25, 53, 116, 117.

Under the Lone Star Flagstick. Hauser, Melanie. 37.

USGA Green Section Record. Wynn, Steve. 103.

Ken Venturi's Stroke Savers. Venturi, Ken. 86, 117.